The Child's World

Published by The Child's World®
1980 Lookout Drive • Mankato, MN 56003-1705
800-599-READ • www.childsworld.com

ACKNOWLEDGMENTS
The Child's World®: Mary Berendes, Publishing Director
The Design Lab: Design and page production
Red Line Editorial: Editorial direction

LIBRARY OF CONGRESS CATALOGING-IN-PUBLICATION DATA
Heinrichs, Ann.
  Punctuation / by Ann Heinrichs ; illustrated by Dan McGeehan and
David Moore.
    p. cm.
  Includes bibliographical references and index.
  ISBN 978-1-60253-433-9 (library bound : alk. paper)
  1. English language--Punctuation—Juvenile literature. I. McGeehan,
Dan, ill. II. Moore, David, ill. III. Title.
  PE1450.H3673 2010
  428.2'3—dc22   2010012344

Printed in the United States of America in Mankato, Minnesota.
July 2010
F11538

ABOUT THE AUTHOR

Ann Heinrichs was lucky. Every year from grade three through grade eight, she had a big, fat grammar textbook and a grammar workbook. She feels that this prepared her for life. She is now the author of more than 100 books for children and young adults. She has also enjoyed successful careers as a children's book editor and an advertising copywriter. Ann grew up in Fort Smith, Arkansas, and lives in Chicago, Illinois.

ABOUT THE ILLUSTRATORS

Dan McGeehan spent his younger years as an actor, author, playwright, cartoonist, editor, and even as a casket maker. Now he spends his days drawing little monsters!

David Moore is an illustration instructor at a university who loves painting and flying airplanes. Watching his youngest daughter draw inspires David to illustrate children's books.

Why should I?

TABLE OF CONTENTS

What Is Punctuation?

why are you running so I can get faster stronger and tougher

Wait a minute. That doesn't make sense! Try this:

Why are you running? So I can get faster, stronger, and tougher!

What makes that better? We added **punctuation marks**:

a **question mark** ?

commas ,

and an **exclamation point** !

Those are just three kinds of punctuation marks. Other dots, squiggles, and dashes have important jobs, too. No matter what it looks like, punctuation shows how words go together.

Wait for me?

Fine, I will!

Stop That Thought.

A **period** . is just a little dot. But it's still important.
A period shows where a sentence ends. A sentence
is a complete thought. It makes sense all by itself.

Without periods, all your thoughts would run together.

Sparky is barking now I can't sleep

You need periods to show where each thought ends.

Sparky is barking now. I can't sleep.

Sparky is barking. Now I can't sleep.

Ask Me Anything

Why can't you clean your room?

When will lunch be ready?

Where did the monster go?

These sentences are questions. Each ends with a question mark ? . A question can be just one or two words. Even short questions get question marks.

9

Yuck! Wow! Yippee!

Watch out!   I won!   I'm so excited!

An exclamation point ! is perfect when you want to express a lot of feeling. It goes at the end of a sentence instead of a period.

Interjections and commands may get exclamation points, too.

Eat your green beans!

Yum!

11

Take a Break

Meanwhile, all the cows escaped.

If we want to win, we have to be tough.

Uncle Jack, who is 90 years old, loves to swim.

Whiskers, my cat, is staring at the bird.

I like cake, but I do not like chocolate.

Commas , break up sentences into smaller parts. Read the sentences above out loud. See how you pause a little at each comma? Commas make sentences easier to read.

Making Lists

The flag is red, white, and blue.

Search in the doghouse, under the bed, and on the deck.

Would you like cookies, cake, candy, pie, or fudge?

Commas are useful for making lists, too. If you want to list three or more things, use a comma between each one.

Missing Letters

Let's go out and play.

Sorry, I haven't eaten yet.

Let's and haven't are **contractions**. A contraction combines two words by leaving out some letters. Let's is short for let us. Haven't is short for have not.

In a contraction, an **apostrophe** ' takes the place of the missing letters. An apostrophe looks just like a comma. The difference is where you find it. An apostrophe goes near the top of a letter. A comma goes near the bottom.

two words	contraction
what is	what's
it is	it's
we will	we'll
you would	you'd
do not	don't
let us	let's

Don't go!

I won't!

The Monster's or the Birds'?

Apostrophes do other things, too.

Have you seen the monster's tricks?

No, I've only seen the birds' tricks.

An apostrophe can show who or what owns something.

the monster's tricks = the tricks of the monster
the birds' tricks = the tricks of the birds

"Were You Speaking?"

"I'm tired today," said the monster.

"What would you like for dinner?" asked Mom.

Quotation marks " " show exactly what's been said. They always come in pairs. Open quotations " come at the beginning of the speech. Closed quotations " come at the end.

20

(And Here's Another Point)

My best friend (besides Sparky) is Emma.

Parentheses ( ) let you explain something or give extra facts. You can add a quick thought inside your sentence. Parentheses always come in pairs. See how much punctuation helps you do? How many different kinds of punctuation can you find on this page?

I like broccoli (but only with cheese sauce)!

How to Learn More

AT THE LIBRARY

Berger, Samantha. *When Comma Came to Town*. New York: Scholastic, 2004.

Bruno, Elsa Knight. *Punctuation Celebration*. New York: Henry Holt, 2009.

Herman, Gail. *Peddling to Perfect Punctuation*. Pleasantville, NY: Gareth Stevens, 2009.

McClarnon, Marciann. *Painless Junior Grammar*. Hauppauge, NY: Barron's Educational Series, 2007.

Pulver, Robin. *Punctuation Takes a Vacation*. New York: Holiday House, 2003.

Schoolhouse Rock: Grammar Classroom Edition. Dir. Tom Warburton. Interactive DVD. Walt Disney, 2007.

ON THE WEB

Visit our home page for lots of links about grammar: *childsworld.com/links*

NOTE TO PARENTS, TEACHERS AND LIBRARIANS: We routinely check our Web links to make sure they're safe, active sites—so encourage your readers to check them out!

23

Glossary

apostrophe (uh-POSS-truh-fee): A punctuation mark that shows to what or whom something belongs or takes the place of the missing letters in a contraction. The apostrophe in *Ella's cat* shows the cat belongs to Ella.

commas (KOM-uhs): Punctuation marks that break up parts of a sentence. Commas make sentences easier to read.

contractions (kun-TRAK-shuns): Contractions are two words combined with some letters left out to make a shorter word. In contractions, an apostrophe shows where letters were left out.

exclamation point (ek-skluh-MAY-shun POINT): A punctuation mark that comes at the end of a sentence and shows surprise. An exclamation point goes at the end of some sentences in place of a period.

interjection (in-tur-JEK-shun): A word that gets attention or shows feelings and stands alone in a sentence. *Hello!* and *Wow!* are interjections.

parentheses (puh-REN-thuh-seez): Punctuation marks used to set off words in a sentence. Parentheses are always used in pairs.

period (PIR-ee-ud): Punctuation mark used at the end of most sentences. A period shows where the end of the sentence is.

punctuation marks (pungk-choo-AY-shun MARKS): Written marks that make the meaning of a sentence clearer. Commas and exclamation points are punctuation marks.

question mark (KWESS-chun MARK): Punctuation mark that shows a sentence is a question. A question mark goes at the end of a question in place of a period.

quotation marks (kwoh-TAY-shun MARKS): Punctuation marks used to show words someone said. Quotation marks are always used in pairs.

Index